D0917268

THE STONES REMEMBER

THE
STONES REMEMBER:

Native Israeli Poetry
Edited by
Moshe Dor • Barbara Goldberg • Giora Leshem

The Word Works
Washington, DC

Printed in the U.S.A.
Typography by Kathryn E. King/Dual Design.
Cover Art: *Cuneiformes #1*, oil, sand, acrylic and fabric on canvas. 45 by 57 inches. 1962, by Moshe Castel. Reproduced with permission of the artist and the University Art Museum, University of California, Berkeley. Book design by Ronna Hammer.

Library of Congress Number: 90-070198
International Standard Book Number: 0-915380-25-0

ACKNOWLEDGMENTS

Publication of the poems in this anthology was made possible by the generous assistance of the Institute for the Translation of Hebrew Literature, Ltd., Tel Aviv, and by ACUM Ltd. in obtaining rights to many of these poems. All rights to the original Hebrew poems are held by each author. © Institute for the Translation of Hebrew Literature for translations by Hillel Halkin of Aharon Almog and Aryeh Sivan; Bat-Sheva Sheriff and Jon Silkin of Anadad Eldan; Dorothea Krock Gilead of Zerubavel Gilead; Gabriel Levin of Varda Ginossar, Yosef Sharon and Ronny Someck; Harold Schimmel of Esther Raab; and Edna Sharoni of Aharon Shabtai. © *Ariel*, the Israel Review of Arts and Letters, for translations by Jay Shir of Na'im Araidi; Judith Dickman of Yehudit Kaffri; and Aloma Halter of Asher Reich. © *Folio* for the translation by Barbara Goldberg of Shlomo Avayou. © Indiana University Press for translations by Warren Bargad and Stanley Chyet of Meir Wieseltier and Chaim Gouri. © *Jerusalem Quarterly* for the translation by Richard Flantz of Shin Shifra. © *Jewish Quarterly* and Mosaic Press for translations by Barbara Goldberg of Moshe Dor. © *Poet Lore* for translations by Jean Nordhaus of Moshe Ben Shaul; Henry Taylor of Yaakov Besser; and Seymour Mayne of Eytan Eytan. © *Triquarterly* for the translation by Zvi Jagendorf of Zelda. The publisher regrets it could not obtain copyright permissions for poems by Yehuda Amichai, Peretz-Dror Banai and Yitzhak Laor.

The Word Works is grateful for the
generous support of the following patrons:

Daniel and Judith Dassa

Emily Glauber

The Grosberg Foundation

Philip S. Morse

Dita van Westerborg

The poems in this collection were translated from the Hebrew by Warren Bargad, Abraham Birman, Chana Bloch, Stanley Chyet, Judith Dickman, Marcia Falk, Richard Flantz, Lisa Fuegl, Barbara Goldberg, Hillel Halkin, Aloma Halter, Catherine Harnett Shaw, Beate Hein Bennett, Zvi Jagendorf, Dorothea Krock Gilead, Shirley Kaufman, Gabriel Levin, Vivian London, Elaine Magarrell, Seymour Mayne, Stephen Mitchell, Jean Nordhaus, Linda Pastan, Jacklyn Potter, Betsy Rosenberg, Anthony Rudolf, Harold Schimmel, Grace Schulman, Edna Sharoni, Bat-Sheva Sheriff, Jay Shir, Jon Silkin, Henry Taylor, Natan Zach, and Linda Zisquit.

CONTENTS

MOTORCYCLES IN THE DARK

PREFACE

The Judean desert lies under a glaring sun. The light, reflecting off coppery rocks, blinds. Thousands of years ago the prophets walked here, listening for the voice of the Lord.

To the east is the Dead Sea, the lowest place in the world. Its waters are heavy, oily. Salt congeals in the crushing heat. Minerals reek. It is easy to imagine the destruction of Sodom and Gomorra in this god-forsaken, foul-smelling region.

The Jordan river, green and lush with beds of reeds, rolls down to the Dead Sea. The river is not wide, and in summer there are certain areas that can be forded on foot. This is the river the Israelites crossed to enter the Promised Land.

Native Israelis identify with biblical stories. We dwell among historical landscapes—the rose of Sharon, and the lilies of that valley, bloom, after all, on Tel Aviv's doorstep. The tamarisks under which Abraham sat are in walking distance from Be'er Sheva University.

Native Israeli Poetry, defined as poetry written by those born in Israel or those who spent their formative years here, is thus stamped with the consciousness of past-as-present. Written in Hebrew, the Holy Language, which went through a marvelous rejuvenation to reemerge as a spoken, living tongue, Native Israeli Poetry uses the landscape as both art and ideology. The great Hebrew poet Shaul Tchernichovsky (1875-1943) coined the phrase, "Man is nothing but the shape of his native landscape." Native Poetry vindicates that concept.

Native Poetry is first and foremost concrete. But it is no dull inventory. Nor does this "indigenous" poetry turn its back on the greater world. But Native poets are psychically and physically bound to specific places, only too well aware of the extremely long and enormously charged history of those places, reverberating with all their cultural associations. Native Poetry, therefore, strains to express the significance of those landscapes. The Bible, the source of Hebrew language and mores, serves as our primary inspiration. At the same time, that heritage is an immense burden with which we must struggle in order to forge our own style. Naturally, Native Poetry is a battleground, an arena of constant strife, as it tries to convey old and new, tradition and rebellion, affluence and poverty, permanence and transition.

"Place of fire/ place of weeping/ place of madness"—thus the poet Zelda defines Jerusalem, the heart of Israel. That metaphor holds true for the entire country. From its very inception, in the biblical-prophetic stage, Hebrew poetry has been a poetry of historic responsibility. Our greatest poets, the prophets, reported to a national conscience even when waxing lyrical. An intimate poem is simultaneously a harbinger of a collective dream.

This complex human and artistic situation is stamped with tragedy. Israeli poetry has war as a major element. Pain, loss, disappointment, grief—all are familiar guests in the house of Israel. The Bible presents forty years as the maximum duration of peace in a land where rival peoples clash for supremacy. Aryeh Sivan knows that during those forty years, "men walk in peace, like sleepwalkers/ in fields of vines and pinetrees." The peaceful days are a hallucination, brief and intangible.

Unceasing bloodshed, like an ancient curse, and the stubborn, almost lunatic, craving for peace, pervade Native Israeli Poetry: "I'm walking in a town where pain, like a good host/ opens the gates/ welcomes quietly, why not, another pain," writes Chaim Gouri. Hope doesn't die. Out of the flames, like the legendary phoenix, poetry rises time and again, linking the Israeli present to the ancient Hebrew past. The first sabra woman poet, Esther Raab, states, "Seven times shall I steep myself/ into the Mediterranean/ to prepare for King David, my beloved,/ and I shall sit with Deborah under the date tree,/ have coffee with her and talk/ about war and defense." Esther Raab, born on the threshold of the twentieth century in the Sharon Valley, fuses with the prophetess Deborah, who led the children of Israel in a triumphant war against the Canaanites and gave us the Song of Deborah, a glorious Hebrew paean of courage and victory.

Israel—land of priests and prophets, judges and kings, destruction and redemption. Land of dreamers and survivors, messiahs and heretics, soldiers and scholars, where "the fig grows here with so much precision/ as though it had grown fully once before" (Yisrael Eliraz). Where smoke still drifts over Sodom, while in Tel Aviv the latest fashions are vaunted in cafés. Where under the heels of commuters, beneath the cement, bones of Canaanite, Philistine, Hebrew, and Arab fertilize the Promised Land.

Israel—where each stone is steeped with history. And the stones remember.

—MD

BARRAGE
OF
BIRDS

התאנה

הַתְּאֵנָה צוֹמַחַת כָּאן בְּדִיּוּק רַב כְּכָל הָאֶפְשָׁר
כְּאִלּוּ כְּבָר צָמְחָה כֻּלָּהּ בְּפַעַם אַחֶרֶת
זֶה טֶבַע יָפְיוֹ שֶׁל הָעֵץ הַצּוֹמֵחַ בְּבִטָּחוֹן פָּשׁוּט שֶׁאֵין לְמַעְלָה מִמֶּנּוּ
וְהוּא גָּדוֹל לְאֵין־שִׁעוּר יוֹתֵר מִבִּטְחוֹנִי שֶׁלִּי
הַמַּבִּיט בּוֹ בְּבֵין־עַרְבַּיִם זֶה וְאוֹכֵל מִפִּרְיוֹ הַמָּתוֹק
שֶׁמָּתוֹק מִמֶּנּוּ רַק דְּבַשׁ הַמַּחֲשָׁבָה עַל אֵינְסוֹפִיּוּת
כָּל נִסְיוֹנוֹתָיו לָשׁוּב וְלַעֲבֹר פֹּה וְלִצְמֹחַ אוֹתָהּ
צְמִיחָה אוֹתָהּ קְלִפָּה עוֹד קְלִפָּה
אֵשׁ בְּתוֹךְ אֵשׁ לֹא תִּכְבֶּה

Yisrael Eliraz

THE FIG

The fig grows here with so much precision
as though it had grown fully once before—
that's the very beauty of the tree, to grow in simple self-assurance
unsurpassed, there's nothing like it and how much more than mine it is
looking at it in this twilight and eating from its sweet fruit,
sweeter is only the honeyed thought of its everlasting
effort to return here again and again and to grow
the same growth, same skin, another skin,
fire within fire never to be extinguished.

translated by Beate Hein Bennett

Natan Yonatan

THE WAY OF ALL FLESH

This primeval dust. Waves pour through the pine forests,
a distant noise screams to you like fields fleeing
in the dark. These southern wadis, names of friends retained
in stone, these winds which razed entire cities and buried
their names under rocks and sand. Unfinished stories
of love left behind in hasty bivouacs between the Zoueira
and crumbling chalks of marl. Many things were lost
to us, unknowing like birds in a storm until they finally
calmed and closed their wings the way of all flesh in rain
that pours obliquely in forests, in caves of stillness
in the way of primeval dust, in the stones, the sea.

translated by Richard Flantz

Moshe Dor

LOCAL FLORA

The Israeli Oak
is Israeli. The Gilboa Iris
grows exclusively on Mount Gilboa:
not just any tree or any flower,
but distinctively native. Indeed
the Israeli Oak (*Pistacia Palaestina*)
and the Gilboa Iris (*Irus Hayeni*)
are from a world view, nearly
unknown, and as to the specificity
of their locale, that has borne
dire consequences: on the Gilboa
that day most likely extravagant
with irises, King Saul fell
onto his sword, suffering mightily
until the young Amalekite slew him,
and while riding under the boughs
of a great oak, Absalom and his
abundant hair became entangled
in a terrible trap of love
from which there was no letting go.

translated by Barbara Goldberg

Na'im Araidi

RETURN TO THE VILLAGE

I returned to the village
where I first learned to weep
I returned to the hill
where distances are green
and no one has use for a picture
I returned to my house of stones
hewn by my grandfathers out of bedrock
I returned to myself
and that is what I wanted.

I returned to the village
having dreamed of a difficult birth
of the word *za'atar** erased from my poems
and of a birth more difficult still
of cornstalks in the deep abandoned earth—
for I had dreamed of the birth of love.
I returned to the village
where I had lived in my last incarnation
out of my roots sprang ten thousand vineyards
upon the good earth
until the wind arose
and blew me far away and returned me
reincarnate and penitent.

Oh, my thirty-second dream:
here were the paths that are no more
and houses grown up like the Tower of Babel
of this heavy dream of mine—
nothing can sprout from your roots!

---

*An aromatic mixture of wild oregano and other herbs native
to the land of Israel; used to flavor a number of Arab dishes.

Where are the children of poverty
ragged as fallen leaves?
Where is my village that was,
where the old paths' names
have been taken by tarmac roads?
Oh, my little village that was once,
swollen now into civilization—
I returned to the village
where the barking of dogs has died away
and the dovecote has become an electric tower.
All the peasants I would sing with,
sing haying songs in nightingale's voice,
are workers now with smoke in their throats.
Where are all those who were, who are no longer?

Oh, this heavy dream of mine—
I returned to the village
running from civilization;
came to the village
as one who goes from exile into exile.

translated by Jay Shir

Giora Leshem

ON THE WAY TO JOB'S POOL

The sun, topsy-turvy, shining beyond
the lake, in the water, in the stream,
and I creeping in light as though
in childhood, from one tip of moss
and basalt to another, transparent,
having already shed the webs
between my toes. This is not
how I remember mornings at Tabha.

In the black stoney niche
at Job's pool, *Hammam el Ayoub*,
in this bitter water, I am immersed
in anxieties, the way crabs
as water rises, extend their legs
out of their shells and move them
like moths in sulfurous salty haze
fishing for whatever comes near.

In this bitter water, I dig
my head in the mud the way
a water crow, flatheaded coracinus,
mustachioed fish digs for mollusks
and crabs, wailing whenever
it is pulled from the water.

Down here, in the subterranean fountains
of sulfur, chlorine, salt, the Galilee
crab has lost its eyes and the color
of its armor, crawling in eyeless terror
in the mud of a lost continent.

They say this species doesn't exist
anywhere else. *Typhlocaris Galileae.*
In Hebrew, only a blind Galilean crab,
nearly extinct. As if a Latin name
could dignify survival and anxiety.

translated by Barbara Goldberg

Aryeh Sivan

JULY 21, 1904

The announcement of Herzl's* death
travelled along the telegraph wires with boundless
speed, with the speed
of the trains between Vienna and Berlin, say,
and when the passengers stepped down
from the train, expiring arbors and woods
into the summer skies, their path
to the telegraph agency was blocked by Jews
who had come to sob a dream.
—Move over, Jew, growled
the telegram clerk, put some kind of
stop to your sorrow.

And in Eretz Yisrael**
a few born in the villages jumped on their horses
and galloped: sons of Rishon
dashed toward the dunes until the sea stopped them in their tracks
and the sons of Gedera galloped eastward to the mountains,
with great speed, as if they were asking
to be torn from the dream
at any moment.

The despairing
grabbed rifles, erected
opposite them the dream like an unsuccessful
clay pot, or a spoiled watermelon, and fired.
In vain: the watermelon seeds, needing no more
than a little dust, absorbed the jets of water
and started a new life cycle.

---

*Theodore Herzl (1860-1904), founder of the Zionist movement.
**Land of Israel.

A country whose laws are the laws of dream
will make watermelons until the telegrams
of condolence arrive.

translated by Gabriel Levin

Aryeh Sivan

ONE HUNDRED YEARS OF
JEWISH SETTLEMENT LATER

Two things there were that puzzled the first settlers in
    Palestine
when, walking to their colonies, they passed
an Arab village, Beidejen, for instance,
and saw its prickly pears, they were amazed
how, in the dry midsummer heat, when nothing green
was left upon the earth, these thorny hedgerows
were still water-soused, just like the camels,
whom the desert did not faze one bit.
(One hundred years of Jewish settlement later
most of these cactus plants have been uprooted
by housing projects blinking in the sun.)

Yet the land snails haven't changed at all.

All the long summer they cling, the snails,
to the thistles' stems
like tiny Arab kaffiyehs, thousands of them.
What are they waiting for? That seems obvious.
They are waiting for the rains to come
and soften, as the winter nears, the ground
that has been stricken by a sudden, strange imperviousness.
Yet why is it that they cling to these dead stems
which offer not even the ghost of a drop of water?

How long can they survive such parchedness?
How do they feel when once again the earth
is sodden with rain? How do they multiply
so much when all is so inexorably dry,

so that in autumn they proliferate
on every weed and thornbush, in every place
not bulldozed by the wheel or tractor tread?

One hundred years of Jewish settlement later
I, for one, don't know.

translated by Hillel Halkin

Avner Treinin

POTASH

In his snow-covered city, my father saw an East
flickering like a *narghila*.* He would lay his head
in a tent in *Palestina. Who is this that cometh dark*

and comely out of her bath with her companions?
Fifty-eight years the sun blazed from the east,
long after the last of his vision had melted.

Most of his life in hard labor,
seventeen years at the Dead Sea, a scorching
solution of potash, a pillar of cloud

of bromide in front of the camp, like the smoke
that rose out of Sodom. Sometimes staring over
the heap, he'd wonder: a wasteland of snow or potash?

translated by Shirley Kaufman

---

*oriental water pipe

Zerubavel Gilead

IN THE VALLEY OF SHILO*

I have been absent from these hills
a long time:
eternal green hills
on which the autumn vine drops
its golden leaves.

Even when a man wanders far
to the great cities of the sea
beyond the green line
his spirit yearns for his own Shilo.
The child hears his name called,
and no one is with him
no one
in the darkness.

Sky-blue on the shoulders
of a golden vine.
Yellow-green leaves, their purple sinews
tracing out a heart,
quiver on his chest.

translated by Dorothea Krock Gilead

---

*"For the Lord revealed himself to Samuel in
Shilo by the word of the Lord" (1 Sam. 3, 21).

Chaim Gouri

OF THE AZAZMEH TOO

And of the Azazmeh* too, it would seem,
freckling the stony vastness
a shadowy intrusion into the realms of the sun.

The Azazmeh, a stink of goats, camels, tar,
the women necklaced, veiled,
opened up in girlhood.

A land of milk and honey and grain in seven kinds,
a land of mule and donkey cocks in summer heat.

The sun, the whole sun, nothing but the sun
and fierce desert winds
and a life gone limp.

And the bearded seers,
they of the torn feet,
their eyes divine embassies.

And the cliff clawing at the sky
and the soul weeping its secret tears.

translated by Warren Bargad and Stanley Chyet

---

*Azazmeh (also Azaazame): One of the Bedouin tribes, living
mainly in the Sinai Peninsula.

16

Esther Raab

HOLY GRANDMOTHERS IN JERUSALEM

Holy grandmothers in Jerusalem,
may your virtue protect me.
The smell of blossoms and blooming orchards
I suckled with my mother's milk.
Feet soft as hands, fumbling
in the torrid sand,
and tousled eucalypti
laden with bees and hornets
whispered a lullaby to me.
Seven times shall I steep myself
into the Mediterranean
to prepare for King David, my beloved,
and I shall go up to him, with glorious dignity,
to the mountains of Jerusalem;
I shall sit with Deborah under the date tree,
have coffee with her and talk
about war and defense.
Holy grandmothers in Jerusalem,
may your virtue protect me.
I can feel the smell of your garments,
the aroma of Sabbath candles and naphthaline.

translated by Abraham Birman

17

Chaim Be'er

TABERNACLE OF PEACE

In Kerem Abraham
Ada with the right hand of her righteousness
bakes cookies from the dust of the earth,
rejoicing in the world of His earth.
A little girl three or four years old
sitting in a sandbox in the morning
in the place where a century ago
the children of ancient and proud families
used to clear stones
and build unhewn stone walls under the guidance of the villagers
in the field of the missionary Mrs. Finn:
young Jews from the Old Settlement
who for their daily bread
earn three and a half piastres
from the wife of the English consul,
touching the Christian heart
by their strangeness and fragility,
and already several vines have been planted
and some mulberry trees
in the heat of the sun
in the yard of the Rachel Strikovsky Kindergarten
where I now see
Hebrew women yawning and sneezing,
holding their children by the hand
in the shade
beneath the mulberry trees,
for in Salem also is His tabernacle.

translated by Stephen Mitchell

Esther Ettinger

MY YARD

This is my yard.
Near the house, grass grows now
and the poppies are on fire and rockrose
shrubs are on fire, the grass is on fire
and a barrel is lying on its side and rust
of several dustbins which know how to sing
a song of worthless things.

And a pair of fig trees, modestly drawing
their cheeks closer to each other and the light,
swaying among the branches.

Even Jerusalem surrounding it
doesn't outshine my yard today with her jewels—
restraining herself, she lets it be.

This is my yard
where I play.

translated by Jacklyn Potter

Yair Hurvitz

AND STILL I LOVE

And still I love. And still I sit hidden.
And still I don't know. And still I don't know what.

What like amazement. I saw a face in sudden amazement.
And still I love. And still I'm not there and I

saw wonders in the look of a face. Fabulous corruption I saw
and still I love and still in fabulous embroidery I'm her captive.
And still I love wonder that bears her corruption great
as suffering and still I love and my mother
from out of my dream bursts forth, my mother from out of my house

and still I love and still my hands like blossom
and the wind caresses me in its sweetness and is gone and still love
and still kingdom.

                                        translated by Harold Schimmel

20

Yehudit Kaffri

SHREDS OF EMBROIDERY

Shreds of colored Bedouin embroidery
fly in the wind between the camels
on the bright hills. Perhaps someone
will try to gather them, to put them
together, but I see
there's no hope. Too pretty,
too torn, they will descend
in the evening, like the wind's
desperately tender bite
on the darkening hills.

translated by Judith Dickman

Moshe Ben Shaul

WIND IN THE HILLS

Wind in the hills rustles, unraveling the hills' voices,
    and I see orchids
swaying like small boats, murmuring like distant oars.
I don't see them white. But like my heart. Beyond the
    abyss. At the edge of throbbing
fog, in multiple sketches of sky, in the fog, silently
    shaken.
And the hills give wind wing when blowing dies away.
    Echoes rise and fall
to the end of moaning.
I touch the earth and milk spills.
Not a day passes, not a solitary frame, not dusk,
because, as in those nights
of the moon's fragmentation, as in a fractious forest
    clearing, milky skies drip, and then
greenish stars like wild grapes oozing and faint wind
within those depths.
Men won't grasp for what they can't afford, a wind blows
    from the days of their childhood, orchids and chopped
pine-nuts at the mouths of fox-pits. And I
see them, and they ask: wind in the hills?

translated by Jean Nordhaus

Leah Snir

NETTLETIME

Perhaps because I broke free
of his authority, the taste
came from an unexpected source,
stubborn summer birds resisting
the cold's directive, the migratory
impulse, seducing light into huts
of musty shade, a wondrous garden
beneath Latiffa's skirt, Latiffa
from Tamrah, her warm fingers encircling
the nettle's searing roots
in the no man's land behind
the nature lab, collecting
nettles in a rough sack swollen
with schemes buried under the gravel
we flung at her to drive her out
of our territory. Tonight
she will brew nettle soup, bitter
with humiliation, sprinkled
with dark spices to arouse
wet birds bathing in her man's
loins. Under the mandrake's spell
he will come unto her as Jacob
came unto Leah, bewitched
by the wild phantasms of nettletime.

                    translated by Barbara Goldberg

Asher Reich

ON A WALK BY THE YARKON

Sumach leaves and my eyes mossy, releasing
a conspiracy of passion
the heart stealthily milling expectations
shadows rise and the smell of the river at night
a fecundity of silence between trees of blossoming wings
and I hear: the earth moves not only our feet
the time the place the body bursting with possibilities
facing terraces of water rushing in wait for us
while talking a chance sensual friction
a sweet journey into the craving blood
half-way there she refuses to continue what's up
what's happened who's looking what's lurking where's the dust
without feigned alarm just a lucid calm
the amenities a minor detail.
The end was something stirred up
that won't be forgotten.

translated by Aloma Halter

Ayin Hillel

AT THE KEFAR SAVA CIRCLE

And on the Fifth of Adar,* buffeted by a world flower storm,
I was hurled at its petals, lashed by merry perfumes.
Water chimes rang out my name, garlands of light called
     Here! Over here!
thinking I was a butterfly, or was it my soul they invited?
     What is the difference?
And the world was innocent as I, but brighter
because of yesterday's rain which also washed off
     the sparrows of freedom.
It was the Fifth of Adar at the Kefar Sava Circle.
or maybe another time and place—

Orchards rushed by, making up oranges, joke after joke,
regaling me so I'd lose my head to laughter.
But I escaped, blue and transparent, into the sky's ten thousand
     dances.
Then, seeing I was a V.I.P. ho-ho!, no, I was God,
the flowers offered to help me to earth again.
I was so important. Because I poked fun at him
even a silly rooster was king.
I was crazy with gaiety!
A persistent jackass walked the road. Laughing,
I questioned my soul: How, on such a day, can persistence be
     entertained?
My soul smiled back. "Only a jackass behaves that way."

Looking out I imagined the land running away like a
     startled cow.
In fact, two cows, Dutch and Damascene, hotfooted it with me to
     Kefar Haro'eh

---

*The sixth month of the Hebrew calendar.

where we were set upon by the flowering
and the orchards confounded us with a tempest of scent,
        thrust us into the sweetest bouquet.
I sighted a flock of boisterous swallows drunk on the cloud
        of perfume.
Hello to my giddy flock of feelings!

The cows, my willing companions but lacking politeness, expansively
        mooed at the world.
How difficult not to moo, also.
I wanted so much to do so after passing the Kefar Sava Circle
because on one of the puddles a haughty duck floated,
mocking the sun in her pond, thinking she caught it!
                        I thought so as well.
How delicious to be silly and know it.
We were ecstatic. The world, ridiculous as it could get.
We hopped up and down.
Was I smiling?
Someone was. Maybe the world. Or the two of us united.

I wanted to taste the air's music, perfumes and voices,
to take a bite with discriminating eyes. Oh, my soul!

Ecstasy was so possible.
Surely I seemed ridiculous to the books in my knapsack,
but what do books know of the world outside on the Fifth of Adar
        at the Kefar Sava Circle!
What do they know of foot races between yellow groundsels and red
        anemones close by the wet athletic field?
What do they know of excursions by electricity so excited
        it bursts its wires?

How ridiculous to be books on a day like this,
a day when one can fall victim to sudden flowering,

breathe with hundreds of frightened senses,
succumb to the clashing of all the world's cymbals!

Oh, on the Fifth of Adar at the Kefar Sava Circle, to be so
    alive!
                    to be
            to be! and to be!

translated by Elaine Magarrell

Yona Wollach

A DENSE AZURE

A dense azure stands in the poplar leaves
and a great light rests on the roses' latticework,
two pepper trees my age are entwined
and branched in each other
tender at my birth, in my honor
ringed with sprinkled gentleness.
Like their blossoms' arrangements
a dark bee's gold floats, zigzagging
going out and up, breezing into the ornaments
ripening, a buzzing rustle full of certainty
quivering and sinking, on the move to float in the face
to bubble with such a bathing love.

translated by Jacklyn Potter

Esther Raab

COCKLEBUR

Cocklebur burst red-loam
and spilled like milk
on earth;
and at night a moon licks
saucers of milk swaying
on slender stalks,
and clouds extend their trail-of-white,
dip in froth of blossoming
flooding cocklebur,
and green bee-eaters in masses
gurgle and go mad
and fill their bellies
with swarming insects
in saucers of white cocklebur;
screw bean surrounds cocklebur
lest it conquer also the sand;
smell of soft screw bean, leaking
and smell of pungent cocklebur leaping—
each on the other with adherence spreading
and filling expanses of flat
red-loam in its clods.

translated by Harold Schimmel

T. Carmi

AS I SIT HERE

As I sit here and think,
the mulberries redden.

Jerusalem is asleep,
and only the water meters are awake.

In the morning I'll open
the kitchen door:
a barrage of birds!

translated by Grace Schulman

Anton Shammas

SITTING ON THE RAIL

Sitting on a Tel Aviv rooftop in the sun
on a cold day. Old pensionaries. A limp
crane tries to lift the town
and the day fallen down into a cup of coffee.

Two cries for help, you and I,
in this sinking city,
sit on the rail
fishing for quiet with love-hooks.

translated by Betsy Rosenberg

Meir Wieseltier

HERE IN NETANYA

Autobiographical Excerpt, 1950–55

We plotted our future, the young city
was old enough for us.
We figured it out: When we were born, she was seventeen.
She could have been our mother.

Some of us were biblical, some were Karl May-niks.*
On the Sabbath we'd wander the dunes northward
over the sea cliffs
a dream ladder cawed to the top of the water tower.
Courageous we climbed, courageous
on the coil of scorching concrete
we glanced sidelong at the sea.
We screamed into the Sabbath silence.

Screams like leaflets from planes
screams upon the dessicated thorns
screams upon the dozing neighborhoods
steaming, know nothing about life.

                    translated by Warren Bargad and Stanley Chyet

---

*Karl Friedrich May (1842-1912) was a popular German author of travel and
adventure serials for young people, tales about Arab desert tribes and
cowboys and Indians.

Aharon Almog

THE SUMMER IS OVER

The summer is over
The streets are over
The shops are over
The squares are over the trees are over
The city is over
The neighborhoods are over
The holidays are over the people are over
The nights are over
The women are over the virgins have fainted away
The end of all flesh
The courtrooms a sabbath for the land
The publishers a sabbath of sabbaths
The newspapers the restaurants
O fallow year the farmers are over
The conferences the meetings the electric power
The best sellers
Are over the cows the milk is over
The fig tree putteth forth its green figs are over
The elections the grapes
The homeowners the walls the flowerpots
The buyers and the sellers are all over.

translated by Hillel Halkin

THAT WOUND
IN THE
EARTH

Chaim Gouri

MAP

Lines. Domes. Ravine. Stains.
Mosque. Furnace. A measured slope.
Sealed mouths of the ovens.
Empty cisterns.   The rock cascade

rising soundlessly toward the underbrush,
toward charred clearings,
toward signs of repentance,
toward the absence of mercy.

Walls of clay without flies.
Wild olives heavy with light.
Yellow scorpions descending
the Way of Tears.

In the torn margins
a fence of warm stones.
Here rest, like old friends
silence
        and fury.

translated by Barbara Goldberg

Yehudit Kaffri

ON THAT DAY

On that day when I walked in the wadi
and found a pure smooth stone that could kill,
on that day when the moon stood still
and the sun froze for six moons
and the smooth pure stone was in my hand
the pure river stone that could kill,
and I let it slip and fall
and that house was still whole,
while I was in the pits of hell
for six months without mercy,
I can't understand why
I didn't throw it at their windows
and that house was still whole
while for six months my life was shattered
and the river stone slipped and fell

and perhaps this is all that's permitted.

translated by Judith Dickman

T. Carmi

AT THE STONE OF LOSSES

> *"There was a Stone of Losses in Jerusalem. Whoever found an object went there, and whoever lost one did the same. The finder stood and proclaimed, and the other called out the identifying marks and received it back."*
> —Baba Metsia 28b

I search
for what I have not lost.

For you, of course.

I would stop
if I knew how.

I would stand
at the Stone of Losses
and proclaim,
shouting:

Forgive me.
I've troubled you for nothing.
All the identifying marks I gave you
(a white forehead,
a three-syllable name,
a neck and a scar,
color and height),
were never mine.

I swear by my life,
by this stone in the heart of Jerusalem,
I won't do it again.
I take it all back.

Be kind to me;
I didn't mean to mock you.

38

I know there are people here
—wretched, ill-fated—
who have lost their worlds
in moments of truth.

And I search
for what I have not lost,
for that—that
name, neck, scar
and forehead white as stone.

    translated by Grace Schulman

Zelda

I STOOD IN JERUSALEM

I stood
in Jerusalem
which hung by a cloud,
stood in a graveyard
with people crying,
a twisted tree.
Blurred hills,
a tower.

You are not,
said death
to us,
nor are you,
he said to me.

I stood
in Jerusalem
that was framed in sun
and smiling like a bride,
stood in a field
near thin green grass.

Why were you afraid of me yesterday in the rain?
said death,
I am your older, your silent
brother.

translated by Zvi Jagendorf

40

Anadad Eldan

THE WORDS THAT SPEAK OF DEATH

The words that speak of death
are frail and blind like chance.
The words that speak of death
drift slow as bubbles
through the fine veins of the heart.

Words you wrote in green
quietly implore
while the sunflower
turns its face.

The words that speak of death
are low as grass.

Wind in the reeds:
it is not words that speak of death.

translated by Anthony Rudolf and Natan Zach

Shin Shifra

ON THE DYING YOUNG MAN

*For Dr. Juan Gackman and Rachel
on the fall of their son, Gabi, in Lebanon*

I
Scent of jasmine and citrus trees
unlocks compassion, Inanna*
is kneeling at the foot of
the apple tree inviting
Dumuzi to make fruitful the grove, someone
from the people of the Chorus, perhaps, is praying for
a cure for the lad, for the summer to delay
its steps, in wordings of spells, why, asks
the stranger, why
must he die because
he touched her nakedness, her *gala*, in Sumerian,
her holy parts, and to me—spring
presages, in the blossomings of citrus,
the stubble and the winter that comes
after the autumn, he will die
in the summer, the boy,
he'll die
in the summer.

II
Inanna, satiated with his loving
in the grove in the shade of the apple,
drains all his strength
and determines his fate, the boy
will die like all the heroes
and afterwards she asks to have

Inanna is the Sumerian goddess of fertility, the Accadian Ishtar.
Dumuzi is the Accadian Tammuz in his Sumerian form.

him placed a star in the heavens, a son
of the heavens, it is fitting for him to be
a star like all the heroes, why asks
the stranger, again blind to the scent
of the blossoms in my nostrils, but they—

III
She says I
dream of what will be
when I wake, a man and a woman
from Argentina, in Kefar Sava the scent
of oranges, citrus
I amend, a man and a woman
from Argentina, jungles and coconut
trees driving every day to Kefar
Sava to visit a cold
stone not believing already a month
has passed, a gentle woman on
the verge of breakdown, I dream
what will be when I wake I don't
want to wake, the bison carried
the boy far off into
the mountains, a bison with spotted eyes
bison with quivering nostrils
with crushing jaws
far away into the fountains the way
that Inanna sings for
the dead Dumuzi.

translated by Richard Flantz

Ra'ya Harnik

I'M NARROWING MY BOUNDARIES

I'm narrowing my boundaries.
Once I was the Land of Israel
I became the State of Israel
Now I'm Jerusalem
Soon I'll be
Mount Herzl
Soon just
You

translated by Jean Nordhaus

---

*Mount Herzl, a national cemetery, includes a military
burial ground.

Eli Alon

BEHIND THE SCREEN

1.
Your whole life you wanted to peek
behind the screen, convinced
you'd find some tenderness
if only you opened the right door
parted the curtain
pronounced the secret code . . .

2.
Like finding a marble hand
thrusting out of the earth

3.
Parting the curtain
opening a door
lifting a stone
and there exposed is the pale nakedness
of the land
your mother's nakedness

4.
The interior of a blue room
the remains of a kitchen, a floor
where a bulldozer has dug
a cesspool

5.
Suddenly
under my son's bed
a chasm gapes:
the sobbing of a Canaanite child

translated by Barbara Goldberg

Dan Armon

LIFTA

On the slope near the highway,
the Arab village destroyed,

graffiti now crowned by wild grasses
scrawled in the deserted rooms—
a refugee or his son stole in,
shouted darkly over the loss of Palestine;

fruit trees of old,
and downstream, the fig trees,

city boys fleeing their books,
lovers under the ruddy pomegranate,

and a carob tree at the threshold
of a room more like a moldy cave—

what a Bar Yochai*
might have dwelt here!

translated by Barbara Goldberg

---

*Bar Yochai, a great Jewish sage, was one of the leaders of the Second
Great Rebellion against the Romans (second century A.D.). According
to legend, he found refuge from his Roman pursuers in a cave whose
mouth was concealed by a carob tree.

Aharon Shabtai

GRANDMA GILA

Grandma Gila, in the silk
so old and black of Sarai,*
a tiny ant at the edge
of the Land of the National Fund.
Beside the shacks of the village latrines,
among my uncles' goats and piles of junk
not far from that wound in the earth, the ravine,
across from which the insane Arab lives.
In the courtyards of the dogs and laundry
she lives conveying nothing more than
awareness of tin tubs and vessels of enamel,
to Canaanite grandchildren who babble a strange tongue
and recoil from the odor of weeping and of nose drops.
Her room had been the Cave of Machpelah**
for many days before the coming of the dog
which bit her to death.

translated by Edna Sharoni

---

*The original name of Sarah, Abraham's wife.
**Where it is believed the Patriarchs and Matriarchs are buried.

Aryeh Sivan

FORTY YEARS PEACE

Forty years peace. Forty years.
Forty years the fig trees
multiply and replenish
the earth, like women whose breasts
touch and get caught everywhere,
and they do not care.
Forty years men sleep with their women:
their breath long and peaceful
like the breath of flutes
in the reeds by small rivers.
They allow the light
of the moon to envelop them:
men walk in peace, like sleepwalkers,
in fields of vines and pine trees.

translated by Anthony Rudolf and Natan Zach

Yaakov Besser

A FIELD STONED

Crushing under my shoe a black mound
of Golan Heights earth and saying: fertile earth.
Counting my reserve service days, I can't forget
Frischmann-Dizengoff corner, a billboard for the Chamber Theater
and you walking by, the jeans stretched over your thighs;
I stare and feel the skin tighten on my cheeks,
grip the binoculars harder and explore
the gray horizon of early winter.
When I examine my fingers, those skilled workers, I see
a flock of white birds soaring (who said wild pigeons
there were dovecotes here only recently). Over a field,
a field stoned. I don't understand
the tractors trying to clear the field,
cultivate it for crops. That earth
under wheat, oats, barley (a soft word).
Funny. But when I look again
at the fingers of my humanity, I lose track
of what's happening to a pit where a stone
lies in its grave. Now a tractor
is trying to uproot it. My fingers
are crushing the earth. My humanity lifts
like a flock of white birds
(anyway who said wild pigeons and the dovecotes)
crossing the border of the Golan Heights. I touch
the jeans stretched over your thighs at the corner
of Frischmann-Dizengoff and survey the gray horizon,
where Mt. Hermon is.
Being born and dying in installments. . . .

translated by Henry Taylor

49

Dahlia Ravikovitch

THE HORNS OF HITTIN

In the morning strange ships appeared on the sea,
prow and stern
in the ancient fashion.
In eleven hundred, bands of crusaders set sail,
kings and rabble.
Crates of gold and plunder piled up in the ports,
ships of gold
piers of gold.
The sun lit marvelous flames in them,
burning forests.
When the sun dazzled and the waves rocked,
they longed for Byzantium.
How cruel and simple the crusaders were.
They plundered everything.

Terror seized the villagers.
These strangers carried off their daughters,
sired them blue-eyed grandsons
in shame,
shrugged off their honor.

Slender-necked ships set sail for Egypt.
The splendid troops struck at Acre,
a lightning force.
All of them swift knights bearing the Bishop's blessing.
A great flock of wolves.

---

*The Horns of Hittin: site of a celebrated battle in which Saladin
decisively defeated the Crusader armies in 1187.

How their eyes shone
when they saw the palm trees sway in the wind.
How they soiled their beards with spittle
when they dragged women into the brush.
They built many citadels,
snipers' towers and ramparts of basalt.
Their bastards in the villages
marvelled at them.

In twelve hundred, the Marquis of Montfort
grew faint.
The winds of Galilee whistled over his gloomy fortress.
A curved dagger burst from the East—
a jester's staff.
Saladin, in motley, advanced from the East.
With a ram's horns that infidel
gored them hip upon thigh,
punished them
at the Horns of Hittin.

No kingdom remained to them,
no life eternal,
no Jerusalem.
How cruel and simple the crusaders were.
They plundered everything.

translated by Chana Bloch

Zelda

PLACE OF FIRE

Mountain air, living air,
breathing lover—
beg mercy for us
from the Most-High.
Place of fire,
place of weeping,
place of madness—
even bride and groom
beg mercy of the heavens
lest the horizon crumble.
Dogs and cats are alarmed.
Only in the plants
the nectars don't darken
a step away from the abyss.
Only in the flowers
the sweetness won't retreat
a step away from death.
For the plants are a different nation
from us,
except for the olive trees
which are sad and wise
like people.
And when a foreign, enemy king
crushes our ties to the city
upon whose neck
a loving prophet hung
sapphires, turquoise, and rubies—
the silver treetops tremble
like my heart.
And when a foreign, enemy king

crushes our awesome love
for the city of David—
the roots of the olive tree
hear a small soldier's blood
whispering from the dust:
The city is crouching on my life.

translated by Marcia Falk

Maya Bejerano

THE HEAT

From above comes the heat: first seen, then arrived, taking
form; whipped into shape.
Grasped in sweaty palms in a changing vaporous haze.
The grass and the brown sand hovered, clinging
to the crotch of Tabor oak branches, the mastic tree.
Their distant slenderness is sunk in the oppressive heat—
melting nests high above.

The chirping expired: a heat cushion strangled their shrieks,
and the defeat that has been troubling me; the fall of the oak.
From inside the empty acorns
insects jumped out in disgust; witnesses of thirst,
far from the source of water.
Poverty of existence and satiety; acorns have been and will be
food for squirrels.
Babies slumber, mothers' breasts;
kiosks distribute clean servings
with hungry flies,
to the seated diners who dropped down onto the steps
of a central station in the field.
Crumbs shining on the edges of mouth and neck.
Bits of gold that hand out heat and light lie uncollected.
We smiled at ourselves; decadence sweeps everything away
like filthy black money; abundance of information and memories;
with no remorse stripping off their covers
into the mix of heat, far from the pendulum clocks,
with no white clothes and drawers of polished vessels.

The waterfall sprays our backs.
Falling into slumber, amid faded grass, swallowed by breath
far from rain and storm and will of volcanoes,
kissing and crying in the heat, bare bellied
and eyelids shading a neck, feet
resting against the heart, the neck, on the neck,

shoulder to shoulder;
the maragosa trees above with claws of shading leaves.
With the slender funnel (transparent) we hear the lashing of the
    sun's rays
without sharp pain things are born,
abandoned and imposed on one another; no parents, no children,
no lover and beloved, and even some haters.
Supine on cotton cloths, wounded with quarreling,
asleep; their interchanging sleep. Bandaged in towels,
their wrists transfuse their dreams to others,
portions of a passing holiday that won't return;
a creature trapped in ironing.
This is the routine obligation to earn a living from some warmth,
among people in a frame of wood and flower,
plaited curtains; there by the hot border, far
away. Unclear if far from here or there. Where to?
The heat will shade (please),
will melt completely, accompany us,
flat in the body and skin,
up in the edge of the cold lakeshore,
in peace.

translated by Lisa Fuegl

Moshe Dor

ASSIMILATION

An evening steamy as a Hassidic bathhouse.
Between your breasts, coastal plain, your sweat
drips like blood which cannot clot. Soon
the incoming breeze will offer a small
consolation. Under the asphalt, bones
of Canaanite, Philistine, Hebrew
and Arab assimilate, and possibilities
forbidden by Mosaic law shall secretly
fertilize the promised land.

                    translated by Barbara Goldberg

Chaim Gouri

CURRENT ACCOUNT

And again, as always in the Land of Israel, the stones boil,
the earth doesn't cover.
And again my brothers are calling from the depths.

Cropped-eared dogs scream in the night
to the passing foreigner
and their brothers answer them.

And again, as always in the Land of Israel,
the headstones are dangerous.
Many of the dozers see a ladder.

The moon is large and rouses
women poets and other moonstruck sleepwalkers
and the ones laying in ambush doze on the crossroads,
as always.

And again, as always in the Land of Israel,
the Gate of Mercy is still locked
and the gravestones are in the shadow of the wall.

And an Elul* sun and mountains dripping nectar
and the hills melting away
and honey flowing.

And again, as always in the Land of Israel,
eyes peek from the palm-shaped charms
and before morning the valley fills with fog
and in the watermelon season the sea is stormy.

---

*Last month of the Hebrew calendar.

And again, as always in the Land of Israel,
the roads hurt from the footsteps of pilgrims
and God feels at home
and my brothers are still calling from the depths.

And fire power
and night power
and a needle that will not pass through
and a feather in the mountains.

And again, as always in the Land of Israel,
the stones remember.
The earth does not cover.
Justice cuts through mountains.

translated by Linda Zisquit

Giora Leshem

HOW IS A RIFT BORN?

A rift is not a living limb
but rather a still-life.
What propels it down a wall, makes it
gravitate to the sides? Like something
alive, it expands or contracts,
breathing with stoney gills
in all the ribs of the house.

Some rifts inhabit the plaster
for years. Invisible, they swell
or dwindle inside the big walls
and at night the house exhales
quietly, bearing the pain
of its fractures.

Sometimes a pale lizard darts
along the lips of a rift,
like a tiny dinosaur, like a tongue
jutting out from behind white teeth.

When I was a child, I remember
hearing about very big rifts.
The Syrian-African fault: a tectonic
disaster, a rip in the basalt heart.
Each night the Jordan bleeds
over the lips of that fault.

translated by Barbara Goldberg

Aryeh Sivan

TO LIVE IN THE LAND OF ISRAEL

To the memory of Tsvi Hurvitz,
pioneer, army commander, and bereaved father.

To be cocked like a rifle, a hand
on your gun, to walk
a tight, hard line, even when
your cheeks have filled with dust,
and your flesh is falling off, and your eyes
can no longer focus on the target.

They say that a cocked gun
is bound to go off. Well, it isn't.
Anything can happen in this Land of Israel.
A broken firing pin, a rusty spring,

or an unexpectedly canceled order,

as was the case with Abraham on Mount Moriah.

translated by Hillel Halkin

MOTORCYCLES
OF THE
DARK

Ronny Someck

ASPHALT: NOSTALGIA POEM

And asphalt is a stitch in the land's garment
a feeling distinguishing between heeltap,
motorcycles of the dark, or a bare foot.
And tonight, the memory of her wet lashes
after showering is similar to the blotch of crows
painted above the eyelid in the asphalt glare.

translated by Gabriel Levin

Moshe Ben Shaul

AS IF A GROVE

Along the road, there is a grove the road cuts across,
its tall palms wilting
under a load of dust
but not the desert, my pretty little sweetheart Tamar.
A shadow dilutes the waning light
that closes down and vanishes.
Trembling air in the wake
of trucks that shake the road.

I said in my heart that little lives wink out;
the air is like that: now living, dead tomorrow.
Yesterday would not have remembered it.

As in a classic play, an ancient hand
drew it out of the archives;
it saw light, and fell asleep again.

When, on the road, you see a grove the road cuts across,
or a vacant lot,
the floating archaeology
melts.

translated by Henry Taylor

Avner Treinin

BEAUTY AT SODOM

1. This beauty is also disappearing.
   The sea is disappearing. The salt heaps up.
   Not finished yet. Not completely Gemmorah,
   Moriah Hotel. One last evening swim in sweet water.
   The bitter water's parting from the earth,
   so foreign, close as water to water.
   Two palms, a few twisted tamarisks.
   So bright. Charred sticks
   to lead you, salt-mushroom picker, in a land
   not an exile-land, not a chosen land,
   more and more on land excised from Sea of
   Death I walk, back to the ancient
   elements: air, earth, wet, hot.

   With no other choice, as when a vein is blocked,
   a plastic bypass without which no blood
   flows, you must get used to it, find a substitute, e.g.:
   How beautifully the sea is disappearing, the salt is heaping up.

2. Don't look back. Even nostalgia, they say,
   is not what it used to be
   and she who used to be is not what you
   thought she was. Look ahead:

   The salt parts from the sea, sea from sea,
   light from skin. Who is that who cometh from the mud?
   They say the mud is full of bromide
   and other brines, there's no cure like it
   for skin diseases, for neuralgia, too.

3. I have passed twenty, forty, fifty, somehow
   haven't been wiped out. Meanwhile, I got rid of Abraham's
   obsession, to seek righteous men here and there.

No fire, no smoke, just a sulphur compound
rises like rot a bit here a bit there.
Sea without fish like fish without sea, without wind

it bubbles, greens, grays, and is swallowed up
in the shadow of mountains behind. In fact,
there is beauty in Sodom, especially if you look back.

translated by Vivian London

Varda Ginossar

THE LEGENDS OF THE KINGS
RETURN TO THIS COUNTRY

In the gray field, shadows on half light,
the field's hair is gold as your eyes are gold, here
where hunting is plentiful, you are enclosed in me,
a river keeping its secrets, a tangle of wonder,
how we do demand to live!

Slowly, the legends, thin as reeds call to us
to tenderly paint them with our lives; we write, we spin, split
wood, draw water

all the forests, all these days becoming
the land, our legs enfolded in the leaves
of the world's book, being read by the sun.

Shemer is the lord of the Mount of Shomron,
a mountain sold in a hasty deal for two talents
of silver, passing through the graceful
hands of a king.

We are bound together, you and I, our muscles
strong as we stand in the mountain's golden hair
like monuments to the fallen, to the risen
and our eyes, like the proud lioness,
grow dim. When we are gone, they will come,

every passerby inhaling silently this rich scent
at the entrance of our house of ancient cypresses,
this tallest mountain, enriched by the earth, bowing
over us to cast a sweet shadow, pour us new wine.

translated by Catherine Harnett Shaw

Eytan Eytan

A KING HELD CAPTIVE
IN WATER TROUGHS

A king held captive in water troughs
His eye the socket of sadness
One night by the sea beyond the dark landscape
at least 70 kms distance over stones
The rising and falling in dense vegetation
A king held captive in troughs
Too weary for sleep, too hurt to keep silent
He falls at first light

With his whole being he has praised the Lord
Full of compassion for shepherds
who herd no more
Raising up a fallen idol, recovering lost wisdom
His eye a fish's caught by the pull of necessity

No more steep descent
No light nor deep fear of light

A place has been found for him, far
from the sweat and stench of his herd

Twisting its way out of him a horrible
noise that turns to a terrifying roar

In the troughs he loses his mind
Let there be light for those
who go forth in darkness

translated by Seymour Mayne

Anadad Eldan

WHEN YOU GAVE LIGHT TO ISRAEL

When you gave light to the sun
And sun to the morning,
I went to you, your only child.

The trees screened the flowing water,
on their branches you hung white birds;
And on me, pupils, dark as my shoes.

Barefooted, the trees are rooted
upright, making God's years green.

Give my legs back those years my father
spent by the swamps that ran here from hillock
to hillock—whistling, hanging his clothes out to dry.

He built a channel for tears; for pain,
shelter in my eyes.

When I see white birds, resting
on the tops of trees, it seems
God or His angels are about.

                    translated by Bat-Sheva Sheriff and Jon Silkin

Yonadav Kaplun

FOR MY DEAR SOULMATES

And again that cry
(though their voices
cannot be heard)—
Follow, follow that voice
until you reach the domain of the Master of Time.
For my dear soulmates who live in Beit Alpha
—and in honor of the Gilboa iris—
here's a little poem in two dozen words
without even a comma damn it:

At the end of time high in the firmament
above the Holy City we'll be depicted
as some heavenly beast
bellowing prophecy and song

                    translated by Seymour Mayne

Mira Meir

IN A SMALL VILLAGE

I would like to sing
of the soft down on your shoulder
the scent of colors between us
the juices of summer fruit
but
we live in a small village.

Wild mustard at my window
pine trees at my window
soft down on your shoulder.
The green field will ripen
and the corn will be harvested.
But
we live in a small village.

translated by Barbara Goldberg

Yaira Ginossar

WITH MY NIECE AT KIBBUTZ YOTVATA

"Native of Israel" is written on the I.D. card
but according to the dates the moon is an immigrant—
a veteran immigrant, in fact,

and in its fullness and set movements
takes responsibility for the timing of Hebrew festivals.
It accompanies me and my hostess

since it too is a kibbutznik
who on the eve of holidays also guides
guests to the communal dining room.

The two of us make it down the footpaths
that are bright as nails in the fingering darkness by the tree
next to the house in Kibbutz Yotvata.

And my hand's in Shai's since I'm her aunt
and she claims me as her own private possession,
pulling me after her
like a big teddy bear.

Like a restless, fluttering butterfly
she leads me
to her friends

who stand tall as an attentive dog
upright on its haunches,
which shakes its shaggy head

and like a sedate old kibbutznik
rejects every bit of bold banter
that reaches its ears.

                              translated by Seymour Mayne

Shlomo Avayou

PEACOCK

Today a peacock was sighted
in the avocado field. Yosef,
the man in charge of irrigation,
spotted it but couldn't catch it.

Imagine! in the field, a peacock,
so close to the noisy coastal highway.
Maybe it escaped from its cage
in the nature lab of a nearby kibbutz.

It certainly can't survive here
with us, Yosef claimed, it's either
martens in the black of night, or
dogs by the light of day.

              translated by Barbara Goldberg

Yisrael Eliraz

THE DESERT

On the border of the scorched grass, there, in the mud, behind a fence,
dark like a pocked woman, in the embroidery of dry leaves
on the tree, dead in the straw, where I climb for observation
out from the moving sage brush—a white surge, at the end of an alley,
like a tunnel—a desert roped in silence,
a rope softer than any soft blue.

I swear like a child that something (to touch it
as it passes by me) is launching out from there,
or maybe floats in the calm destined for big times,
like a pear, July, holding back in the tree.

translated by Beate Hein Bennett

Yosef Sharon

BARRACKS (ZRIFIN*)

Footpaths leading up to the place were blocked.
The shack windows were in fact of unexpected
dimensions, larger than usual,
but the trees nearby obstructed and softened
the partial view: some villas,
red-lidded white containers, plants branching out
along the ground, leading in a straight line
to the depot on which was written in brown:
"Insecticides." One evening they came out,
three toads, from under the wood steps,
after the rain, and found me sitting and smoking
and it was as though they exposed the defect in me:
the patience to listen right to the end
to a puppet show of vexations and rebukes.
None of them actually spoke, everything was hinted
at by gestures of the hand and feet.
One drew its hands up to its eyes and another
pointed to my eyes, as though demanding of me
my sight—not unlike a charming old man
who talking face to face made such a gesture
when he meant to say: we both see the world eye
to eye—the second jumped, leaped lightly
and ran one hand over the other as if pointing
at the length of the gloves it was wearing,
insinuating that it desired my own hands
or fingers, only I wasn't sure if it was pulling
on an imaginary sock intended for my foot
or perhaps it was really a matter of gloves,
intended for my fingers. The third
ran its hand over its head and smoothed down several
swellings (lacking facial bones and consequently

---

*The name for an army camp in the center of the country.

any form of a mask) and then I understood
that it simply wanted my skull.
Nothing less.
With one kick I could have put
an end to the problem, such things don't repulse
me, except that I rapidly realized
how if they spoke from my throat, then surely
they owed me my eyes, my hands, everything.
I didn't kick them. They dove into the small pond,
the puddle, near the shack, by now dark. The skull
seemed to shudder under the skin.

                    translated by Gabriel Levin

Seffi Shefer

IN THE OLD PORT

In the Old Port of Tel Aviv
a doll's head bobs in the water,
rusting pipes grow soft in algae gold.
The sea reclaims its own.

Across from the Old Port—
miraculous fishing boats from Jaffa,
gruff and salty people
cut a short path to the sun.

In the Old Port of Tel Aviv
vines wrap windows
of deserted palaces,
in the Old Port
boundless treasure lies.
And only love's elect can come there
and reclaim their own.

                    translated by Jean Nordhaus

Ortzion Bartana

SIDE-STEPPING

The passersby keep to the edge of the street,
trying to side-step the mountain.

Instead I take the mountain
home with me.

In my room I sit down on its summit
and glimpse the sea.

translated by Linda Pastan

Sabina Messeg

JOB'S POOL HAS BEEN CLOSED DOWN

Job's Pool has been closed down;
you came in vain from Jerusalem with your boils and the pistol;
this is only a scanty flow the Water Authority has left open—
not a gift from the earth!

Yet there is pleasure here:
there is Grass Power
that enters the nose,
and the air is bent over all—
not just in charge of the world.

A crab with a good camouflage
could live well here
        just think;
the world of dampness under the waterfall . . .

translated by Henry Taylor

Varda Ginossar

JAFFA, LOCKING INTO PLACE

Locking the years into place
in a den of transparent fears, like a demon
shackled to his bodily shapes,
a field in my very body lent his shape.

Screw on the face,
the most awful criminals can guard
my small steps,
and in my eyes they were like dream-lion cubs
growling.

Drug-taking is like a demon
whose shapes on their body I've seen, horny
males with exposed members,
and I to the blueness of a shirt
am gathered.

People within people within people,
rooms within rooms within rooms,
fears within fears within fears,
locking the years into place, years like ravens,
there black ones caw on the abandoned pier,
I'm naked now, a fiend shackled in all his bodily
shapes has congealed in my very body.

translated by Gabriel Levin

Eli Hirsch

ORNA IN BETHLEHEM

These days Orna lives in Bethlehem,
a town where shade and sunlight organize
not only color, but space and time;
there a tree speaks, and one house seems to hold
all things—a foreign homosexual
      and felonious hashish, a DJ
      making brute policemen dance;
      and as they dance, they sing:
      "I'm going away,
      please don't leave me,
      let's dance forever, hold me tight.
      Nothing is ever the way it was.
      What used to be is forgotten now,
      and there's nothing left now but tonight."

                translated by Henry Taylor

Mordechai Geldman

CAFÉ

At Café Milano which isn't
in Milano, a Palestinian waiter
prepares coffee for me, he smiles,
black eyes glinting as though
he can read my mind.

Youthful pagan soccer fans
listen to a fat blond guy analyze
plays from the field;
it's evening now but his eyes
still sport purple-tinted sunglasses.

A secret signal eliminates everyone,
the beautiful, heavily made-up waitresses
too. And at a deserted café
I confront a Palestinian waiter.

He sees what I see and I see his eyes.

He sees that my stare is not political.

The secret signal eliminates me too.

On the way home, the dark tender
with electric lights, I see trailing
from a balcony, a tangle of roses.

translated by Barbara Goldberg

Dahlia Ravikovitch

HARD WINTER

The little mulberry shook in the flame
and before its glory vanished
it was lapped in sadness.

Rain and sun ruled by turns, and in the house
we were afraid to think
what would become of us.

The bushes reddened at their hearts
and the pond disappeared.
Each of us was sunk in himself alone.

But for an instant, off guard,
I saw
how men are toppled from this world

like trees struck by lightning
heavy with limbs and flesh, the wet branches
trampled like dead grass.

The shutter was worn and the walls thin.
Rain and sun, by turns, rode over us
with iron wheels.

All the fibers of the plants were intent
on themselves alone.
This time I never thought I'd survive.

translated by Chana Bloch

Zerubavel Gilead

THE TREE

When I touched its trunk
it shook its heavy
leaves
And rubbed my fingers raw.
A beetle, a stranger among
the branches,
stared at me with a thousand crooked
eyes.
And the tree was silent.

My feet
began to shiver
to the soft music of the roots.

translated by Dorothea Krock Gilead

Rubi Schoenberger

ON GUARD

Green grass
grows
on an earth mound
one month old

in the evening it grows colder.

On the way
to the place from which I'll watch
the frightened desert animals
all night,
the foot grows accustomed to a bush, a stone, a knoll;
here even the rift is only
a flat valley.
The smell rising in my nose when I stop.

All I'm going to do till morning:
light a hidden fire
and sleep under cover.

The groans of dream
frighten away
field mice.

You are the highwayman
who frightens
the guard.
Years of
wearisome nights won't erase the memory
of the theft. I still

wake sometimes   get up
wipe the sweat
and give in to suspicious dread

without a house or any shelter, without
the wish to defend myself.

translated by Jacklyn Potter

Moshe Dor

ALTERNATE POSSIBILITIES

Here is the station of alternate
possibilities—one can get off, or
keep on traveling. But a motherland,
is that subject to choice? A man
carries his passport in his breast
pocket because he craves foreign air,
a sky as singular as the ceiling
of a room he has never slept in,
and in his belly he nurtures
exotic birds, possessions
too precious ever to pawn.

It's impossible, a man says
to himself, to be torn in half,
and unhealthy too. Well, he gets off
or he travels on, and suddenly
instead of familiar road, a lake
imposes itself on his vision.
Cattails brush his lips. He runs
and shouts because his heart
is bursting. The entire earth
encompasses him, and all
his blood is contained within.

The poet is condemned to double
vision, but sand and stone are
sand and stone and have been
since the beginning. They lack
the capacity to forgive. The poet
looks at the man begging for mercy,

begging to be made whole, and tries
to crawl to his brother. He sings
his lament, all the colors
of the world in his mouth.

translated by Barbara Goldberg

Chaim Gouri

HOSPITALITY

I'm walking in a town where pain, like a good host,
opens the gates
welcomes quietly, why not, another pain.
To these cries, I can add nothing.
In these times,
all is wounded and all has been said.
And so I walk like a receding danger
talking to alien walls
like a fourth-rate Jeremiah without interpreter.
The blood that crossed these stones before me
long since passed into silence and time.

translated by Jean Nordhaus

Amos Levitan

ROSH PINA

To come as far as Rosh Pina
where even the black basalt
begins, the many-branched eucalyptus;

to come a way of abstinence, submissive,
to this scorched clearing,
to lay your head there, in that final

field of murky light, at the edge
of the embattled earth;
in that land, Rosh Pina,
older than sunrise.

translated by Catherine Harnett Shaw

ABOUT THE EDITORS

MOSHE DOR was born in 1932 in Tel Aviv. He is the author of 25 books, most recently, *Crossing the River.* For many years Dor was on the editorial board of *Maariv,* one of Israel's leading newspapers, finally serving as its literary editor. He has been Counsellor for Cultural Affairs at the Israeli Embassy, London, England, and Distinguished Writer-in-Residence at The American University, Washington, D.C. A former president of the Israeli P.E.N., Dor has received several literary awards, including the Bialik Prize and the Prime Minister's Prize. He is the major proponent of the Israeli Native School of Poetry.

BARBARA GOLDBERG was born in 1943 and raised in Forest Hills, New York. She graduated from Mount Holyoke College, Columbia University, and received her M.F.A. from The American University, Washington, D.C. She is the author of *Cautionary Tales* (winner of the Camden Poetry Award) and *Berta Broadfoot and Pepin the Short: A Merovingian Romance.* The recipient of two fellowships from the National Endowment for the Arts, she received the Armand G. Erpf Award from the Translation Center, Columbia University, for her translations of Moshe Dor's poetry. Goldberg, an executive editor of *Poet Lore* magazine, is director of the editorial board of The Word Works.

GIORA LESHEM was born in 1940 in Tel Aviv. A former computer programmer, he currently writes and edits for the Israeli Press. The recipient of several literary awards, including the Prime Minister's Prize, he has translated D. H. Lawrence and Sylvia Plath into Hebrew. He has published a selection of William Blake's poetry in translation as well as two volumes of his own poetry and a collection of literary essays.

ABOUT THE ARTIST

MOSHE CASTEL was born in 1909 in Jerusalem, the scion of a Sephardi family established there since 1492. Castel studied art at the Bezalel Academy and then studied and worked in Paris from 1927 to 1940, after which he settled in Safed. He represented Israel in the Venice Biennale in 1948 and the Sao Paulo Biennale in 1959. His works include monumental panels in the Knesset building and the President's House in Jerusalem. An exhibit of his selected works was shown in the Knesset in 1984-85.

BIOGRAPHICAL NOTES

AHARON ALMOG was born in 1931 in Tel Aviv where he lives today. He is the author of six volumes of poetry, as well as three novels. A high-school teacher of Hebrew literature, he has been awarded the Prime Minister's Prize and the Brenner Prize.

ELI ALON was born in 1935 on Kibbutz Ein Shemer where he is still a member. He is active in the kibbutz's cultural life, and has worked as a journalist. He has published six books of poetry.

DAN ARMON was born in 1948 in Jerusalem. He holds a Bachelor of Arts degree in Hebrew literature and theater, and is currently an instructor in the Alexander technique. He has published four volumes of poetry.

NAIM ARAIDI was born in the Druze village of Ma'hr in the Galilee in 1950. Having received his Ph.D. in Hebrew literature, he now teaches Hebrew and Arabic literature in teachers' colleges and at Haifa University. A prolific author in both Hebrew and Arabic, he has published critical studies and essays, collections of Arabic verse in translation, and several volumes of his own poetry.

SHLOMO AVAYOU was born in Turkey in 1939 and immigrated to Israel in 1949. He moved to Kibbutz Ga'ash in 1979, and there the former teacher and research assistant has worked in the avocado fields for 11 years. He has published a novel, a collection of short stories, and five volumes of poetry.

ORTZION BARTANA was born in 1949 in Tel Aviv where he lives today. Once the editor of a literary magazine published by Tel Aviv University, he now edits *Moznayim*, the monthly of the Hebrew Writers Association, and teaches Hebrew literature at Bar Ilan and Tel Aviv Universities. The author of books of criticism, he has also published one collection of short stories and four volumes of poetry.

CHAIM BE'ER was born in 1945 in Jerusalem, the son of a family who has lived there for over 150 years. He is a reporter, editor at the Am Oved Publishing House, critic, author and poet. He has published two novels and a collection of poetry, and was a recipient of the Bernstein Award and the Prime Minister's Prize.

MAYA BEJERANO was born in Haifa in 1949 and has since lived all over Israel. She holds a Bachelor of Arts degree in literature and philosophy, has studied violin and flute, and is an amateur photographer. The author of several collections of poetry, she is the recipient of three literary prizes, including the Prime Minister's Prize.

MOSHE BEN SHAUL was born in Jerusalem in 1930 and for some years was a member of Kibbutz Gevim in the Negev. He has been the Israeli cultural attaché in Paris. He has translated French literature extensively, including the poetry of Cocteau and the well-loved *Babar* books for children. A prolific author, he has published numerous volumes of prose, drama, and poetry for both adults and children. He is the recipient of a number of literary prizes, including the Chomsky and Bernstein Prizes.

YAAKOV BESSER was born in Poland in 1934 and immigrated to Israel in his youth. Currently the editor of *Iton 77*, an Israeli literary monthly, he has been a prolific author since his first publication in 1965.

T. CARMI was born in 1925 to a Hebrew-speaking home in New York City. His first volume of Hebrew poetry was published while he was still living in the U.S. Having immigrated to Israel in 1947, he fought in the 1948 War of Independence and then settled in Jerusalem. A recipient of the Bialik Prize, an editor and translator, he is a professor of Hebrew literature at Hebrew Union College in Jerusalem. He has published many collections of his own verse, and translated and edited two anthologies of Hebrew poetry, including *The Penguin Anthology of Hebrew Verse*.

ANADAD ELDAN was born in 1924 in Poland and immigrated to Israel as a young boy. A member of the Palmach, he fought in the War of Independence. The author of nine volumes of poetry, he lives and teaches in Kibbutz Be'eri.

YISRAEL ELIRAZ was born in 1936 in Jerusalem where he lives today. A Jerusalem principal of a high school he holds a Bachelor of Arts degree in philosophy and Hebrew literature, and a Master's degree in Hebrew literature. An author of drama, prose, and poetry, he is the recipient of three literary prizes.

ESTHER ETTINGER was born in 1941 in Jerusalem where she lives today. She holds a Bachelor of Arts degree in literature and Jewish history and currently is a librarian at Hebrew University. The author of three volumes of poetry, she has received three literary prizes, including the Newman Prize for First Publications.

EYTAN EYTAN was born in 1940 in the village of Kinneret, Israel, where he still lives and works as an organic agriculturalist. He is the author of two volumes of poetry.

MORDECHAI GELDMAN was born in Munich in 1946 and immigrated to Israel at a very young age. He lives in Tel Aviv where he is a clinical psychologist. The author of several volumes of poetry, he is also a regular contributor to the Israeli literary press and a recipient of the Chomsky Prize.

VARDA GINOSSAR was born in Egypt in 1943 and was brought to Israel as a baby. She grew up in Jaffa, studied literature, philosophy, and film in Tel Aviv, and currently teaches yoga. She serves as the General Secretary of the Hebrew Writers Association and is the author of three volumes of poetry.

YAIRA GINOSSAR was born in 1938 in Israel and lives in Tel Aviv. She is currently working on her doctorate in Hebrew poetry, which she also teaches. She is the author of three volumes of poetry.

ZERUBAVEL GILEAD (1912-1988) was born in Bessarabia and has lived on Kibbutz Ein Harod since childhood. A member of the Palmach, the crack fighting unit of the Haganah and the fledgling Israeli Army, he was in charge of all its publications and wrote the famous "Song of the Palmach." A writer of both prose and poetry for adults and children, he received the Prime Minister's Prize and the Bialik Prize.

CHAIM GOURI was born in 1923 in Tel Aviv. A member of the Palmach, he served in the War of Independence. He also carried out Haganah missions in Europe after World War II. A recipient of the Bialik Prize and the Israel Prize, he has written numerous volumes of poetry. He is also a novelist, journalist, and film producer.

RA'YA HARNIK was born in Berlin in 1933, immigrated to Israel in 1936, and currently lives in Jerusalem. The editor of documentary programs on Kol Israel Radio, she is the author of two books of poetry.

AYIN HILLEL (1926-1990) was born on Kibbutz Mishmar Ha'emek and spent his later years in Tel Aviv. Jerusalem's chief gardener from 1954 to 1960, he designed Jerusalem's botanical and biblical gardens, and continued to work in landscape architecture after he moved to Tel Aviv. A beloved author of children's literature, he also published several volumes of poetry for adults. He was the recipient of both the Fichman Prize and the Prime Minister's Prize.

ELI HIRSCH was born in Israel in 1962. A literary critic at the weekly *Ha'ir*, he is currently working on his Master's degree in philosophy. He has published one volume of poetry.

YAIR HURVITZ (1941-1988) was born and lived in Tel Aviv. He earned his living as a typesetter and proofreader. His special affinity for Scottish poetry led to his publishing a collection of Scottish poems in translation. During his life, he published eleven volumes of his own poetry, and received the Prime Minister's Prize and the Alterman Prize.

YEHUDIT KAFFRI was born in 1935 on Kibbutz Ein Ha'choresh. She now lives in Mazkeret Batya, where she is a translator and editor in the fields of psychology and education. The author of several books, both poetry and prose, she is a recipient of the Prime Minister's Prize.

YONADAV KAPLUN was born in Australia in 1963 and immigrated to Israel in 1970. He currently lives in Jerusalem, where he studies at a yeshiva. A frequent contributor to Israeli journals, he has published two volumes of poetry.

AMOS LEVITAN was born in 1935 on Kibbutz Kfar Masaryk and currently lives in Tel Aviv. The editor of the literary supplement of the daily *Al Hamishmar*, he holds a Master's degree in philosophy. He has published three books of poetry and is the recipient of the Anna Pollack Prize and the Holon Prize.

MIRA MEIR was born in Poland in 1932 and immigrated to Israel as a young girl. A member of Kibbutz Nachson, she is the editor of books for children and youth at the Sifriat Poalim publishing house. She has published her memoirs, 18 children's books, and four collections of poetry, and is the recipient of a number of literary prizes.

SABINA MESSEG was born in 1942 in Bulgaria and immigrated to Israel in 1948. She has published several books, including translations of English literature and her own poetry in Hebrew.

ESTHER RAAB (1894-1981) was born in Petach Tikva to one of its found-ing families. She lived briefly in both Cairo and Paris. The daughter of a pioneer, she has been termed "the first native-born Hebrew woman poet." During her life she published three volumes of poetry. A complete collection was published posthumously.

DAHLIA RAVIKOVITCH was born in 1936 in Ramat Gan. She studied at He-brew University in Jerusalem and later worked as a journalist and high-school teacher. The translator of a number of English-language child-ren's books, including *Mary Poppins*, and the poetry of W. B. Yeats and T. S. Eliot, she has also published a novel and six volumes of her own poetry. Among her awards is the Bialik Prize.

ASHER REICH was born in 1937 in Jerusalem to an ultraorthodox family. He studied philosophy and literature at Hebrew University in Jerusalem and is a former editor of *Moznayim*. He is the recipient of a number of literary prizes, including the Prime Minister's Prize. Several volumes of his poetry have been published.

RUBI SCHOENBERGER was born in Timisoara, Romania, and immigrated to Israel as an infant. He holds a Bachelor of Arts degree in literature and a Master's in clinical psychology, the field in which he works. He has published one volume of poetry.

AHARON SHABTAI was born in 1939 in Tel Aviv where he lives today. He holds a doctorate in classical Greek and has published a number of translations of Greek literature, including *Oedipus Rex*. He teaches Greek theater at Hebrew University. The recipient of the Prime Minister's Prize, he has published several volumes of poetry.

ANTON SHAMMAS was born in the Arab village of Fassuta, Israel, in 1950. A resident of Jerusalem, he currently teaches at the University of Michigan. For several years a co-editor of an Arabic monthly literary magazine, he has also worked as a producer of Arabic programs for Israel Television and written a weekly newspaper column. He has received a number of literary prizes, including the Prime Minister's Prize. His publications include a novel, *Arabesques*, and three volumes of poetry, one in Arabic and two in Hebrew.

YOSEF SHARON was born in 1952 in Tel Aviv where he still lives. He studied philosophy at Tel Aviv University and has since worked in book publishing and magazine editing. He has published articles, translations, and essays on poetry, as well as two collections of his own poems.

SEFFI SHEFER was born in 1956 in Havatzelet Hasharon, Israel, and now lives in Tel Aviv. She studied Hebrew literature and philosophy at Tel Aviv University and is currently a newspaper copyeditor and book editor. She is the author of two collections of poetry.

SHIN SHIFRA was born in 1931 in Israel. She studied kabbalah, literature, and education at Hebrew University and Tel Aviv University. A teacher of creative writing to high-school students, she also translates Mesopotamian literature into Hebrew. A recipient of the Prime Minister's Prize, she has published a novel and several volumes of criticism and poetry.

ARYEH SIVAN was born in Tel Aviv in 1929. As a member of the Palmach, he fought in Israel's War of Independence. Today he is a high-school teacher of Hebrew language and literature, which he studied at Hebrew University in Jerusalem. He has published nine volumes of poetry and is the recipient of the Prime Minister's Prize and the Brenner Prize.

LEAH SNIR was born in 1945 on Kibbutz Mishmarot, and now lives on Kibbutz Beit HaShita. She holds a Bachelor of Arts degree in comparative literature and Jewish philosophy, and a Master's in Hebrew literature and art history. An editor and critic, she has published three volumes of poetry and was awarded the Wertheim Prize.

RONNY SOMECK was born in Baghdad in 1951, but came to Israel as a young child. With a Bachelor of Arts degree in Hebrew literature and Jewish philosophy, he has worked as a counselor with street gangs, taught literature, and currently leads creative writing workshops. The author of five volumes of poetry, he is a recipient of the Prime Minister's Prize.

AVNER TREININ was born in 1928 in Tel Aviv and has lived most of his life in Jerusalem. In 1950, he completed his doctorate in chemistry and has since taught chemistry and served as Dean of the Faculty of Natural Sciences at Hebrew University. He has also conducted research and taught abroad. The recipient of a number of literary prizes, including the Bialik Prize, he has published stories, articles, and seven volumes of poetry.

MEIR WIESELTIER was born in 1941 in Moscow and immigrated to Israel in 1949. He has co-edited the Israeli literary journal *Siman Kri'a* and was the poetry editor for the Am Oved Publishing House. A translator of English, French, and Russian poetry, as well as of two novels by Virginia Woolf, he has published eight volumes of his own poetry.

YONA WOLLACH (1944-1985) was born in Kiryat Ono, Israel. In addition to her literary endeavors, she wrote for and appeared with an Israeli rock group. In 1982, her poetry was set to music and a record released. Frequently featured in major Israeli literary journals, she also published several volumes of poetry.

NATAN YONATAN was born in Kiev in 1923 and immigrated to Israel as a two-year-old. He has lived and worked on Kibbutz Sarid since 1945. He has taught at high school and university levels, both in Israel and in the U.S. He has been a senior editor of the Sifriat Poalim Publishing House since 1971. He is the recipient of several awards including the Prime Minister's Prize and the Bialik Prize, and has published extensively, including a novel, children's books, and poetry.

ZELDA (1916-1984) was born in the Ukraine and died in Jerusalem. A devout Hassid, she was a teacher by profession. Awarded the Prime Minister's Prize, she published three volumes of her poetry in her lifetime. Her collected poems were published posthumously.

INDEX

OTHER BOOKS IN THE WORD WORKS SERIES:

*Washington Prize winner
**Capital Collection

WORD WORKS ANTHOLOGIES:

Requests for our brochure and other information must be accompanied by a self-addressed stamped envelope.